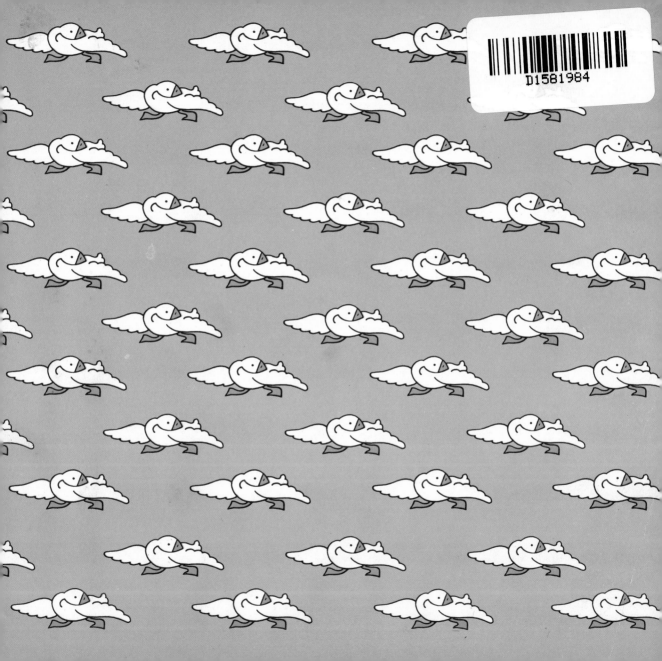

Titles in Series S892

Little Tommy Tucker and other nursery rhymes
Little Jack Horner and other nursery rhymes
Little Bo Peep and other nursery rhymes
Little Miss Muffet and other nursery rhymes

British Library Cataloguing in Publication Data
Little Jack Horner and other nursery rhymes.
  I. Bracken, Carolyn
  398'.8
  ISBN 0-7214-9591-5

First edition

Published by Ladybird Books Ltd Loughborough Leicestershire UK
Ladybird Books Inc Auburn Maine 04210 USA

Printed in England

Little Jack Horner
and other nursery rhymes

Illustrated by Carolyn Bracken

Ladybird Books

Humpty Dumpty sat on a wall,
Humpty Dumpty had a great fall;
All the king's horses,
And all the king's men,
Couldn't put Humpty together again.

Little Jack Horner sat in the corner,
Eating a Christmas pie.
He put in his thumb and pulled out a plum,
And said, "What a good boy am I!"

Oh, dear, what can the matter be?
Dear, dear, what can the matter be?
Oh, dear, what can the matter be?
Johnny's so long at the fair.

He promised to buy me a pair of sleeve buttons,
A pair of new garters that cost him but tuppence;
He promised he'd bring me a bunch of blue ribbons
To tie up my bonny brown hair.

Mary, Mary, quite contrary,
How does your garden grow?
With silver bells and cockle shells,
And pretty maids all in a row.

Pretty maid, pretty maid,
Where have you been?
Gathering roses
To give to the queen.
Pretty maid, pretty maid,
What gave she you?
She gave me a diamond
As big as my shoe.

Cobbler, Cobbler, mend my shoe;
Get it done by half past two;
Stitch it up, and stitch it down,
Then I'll give you half a crown.

Mary had a little lamb,
Its fleece was white as snow;
And everywhere that Mary went,
The lamb was sure to go.

It followed her to
        school one day,
Which was against
        the rule;
It made the children
        laugh and play
To see a lamb
        at school.

And so the teacher
      turned it out,
But still it lingered near;
And waited patiently about,
Till Mary did appear.

"Why does the lamb love Mary so?"
The eager children cry;
"Why, Mary loves the lamb, you know,"
The teacher did reply.

A diller, a dollar, a ten o'clock scholar,
What makes you come so soon?
You used to come at ten o'clock,
But now you come at noon.

One misty, moisty morning,
When cloudy was the weather,
There I met an old man
Clothed all in leather.

Clothed all in leather,
With cap under his chin.
How do you do,
And how do you do,
And how do you do again?

It's raining, it's pouring,
The old man is snoring;
He went to bed,
And bumped his head,
And couldn't get up in the morning.

Doctor Foster went to Gloucester
In a shower of rain;
He stepped in a puddle,
Right up to his middle,
And never went there again.

Daffy-down-dilly is now come to town,
In a yellow petticoat and a green gown.

On Saturday night shall be my care
To powder my locks and curl my hair;
On Sunday morning my love will come in,
When he will marry me with a gold ring.

When I was a little girl,
About seven years old,
I hadn't got a petticoat
To keep me from the cold.

So I went to Darlington,
That pretty little town,
And there I bought a petticoat,
A cloak and a gown.

As I was going to St Ives,
I met a man with seven wives;
Each wife had seven sacks,
Each sack had seven cats,
Each cat had seven kits.

Kits, cats, sacks, and wives,
How many were going
                    to St Ives?

(Answer: Only one – "I")

Six little mice sat down to spin;
Pussy passed by and she peeped in.
What are you doing, my little men?
Weaving coats for gentlemen.

Shall I come in and
        cut off your threads?
No, no, Mistress Pussy,
        you'd bite off our heads.
Oh, no, I won't, I'll help you spin.
That may be so,
        but you can't come in.

Pussy Cat Mole jumped over a coal,
And in her best petticoat burnt a great hole.
Pussy Cat Mole shall have no more milk,
Until her best petticoat's mended with silk.

I love little pussy, her coat is so warm,
And if I don't hurt her she'll do me no harm.
So I'll not pull her tail, nor drive her away,
But pussy and I very gently will play.

My mother said that I never should
Play with the gypsies in the wood.
The wood was dark, the grass was green;
In came Sally with a tambourine.

One, two,
Buckle my shoe;

Three, four,
Knock at the door;

Five, six,
Pick up sticks;

Seven, eight,
Lay them straight;

Nine, ten,
A big fat hen;

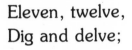

Eleven, twelve,
Dig and delve;

Thirteen, fourteen,
Maids a-courting;

Fifteen, sixteen,
Maids in the kitchen;

Seventeen, eighteen,
Maids in waiting;

Nineteen, twenty,
My plate's empty.

What's the news of the day,
Good neighbour, I pray?
They say a balloon
Is gone up to the moon!

I see the moon,
And the moon sees me.
God bless the moon,
And God bless me.